MIND RENEWAL
TRANSFORMATION DEVOTIONAL Vol. 1

Presented to

_____

By

_____

Date

MIND RENEWAL TRANSFORMATION DEVOTIONAL Vol. 1

A 30-Day Transformation Journey

LEOSTONE MORRISON

Extra MILE Innovators
Kingston, Jamaica W.I.

Copyright © 2019 by Leostone Morrison

ISBN-13: 978-1-62676-647-1

ALL RIGHTS RESERVED

Without limiting the rights under copyright reserved above, no part of this publication may be reproduced, stored in or introduced into a retrieval system, or transmitted, in any form, or by any means (electronic, mechanical, photocopying, recording, or otherwise), without the prior contractual or written permission of the copyright owner of this work.

· · · · ·

Published by
Extra MILE Innovators
21 Phoenix Avenue,
Kingston 10, Jamaica W.I.
www.extramileja.com
administrator@extramileja.com
Tele: (1876) 782-9893

Cover Design by Tevaun Brown
tbartgraphic@gmail.com

Unless otherwise stated Scripture verses are quoted from the New King James Version of the Bible

Author Contact

For consultation, feedback or speaking engagements contact the author at restorativeauthor@gmail.com

PRAISE FOR MIND RENEWAL

A must-read life-changing book. The Bible states the word of God is sharper than a two-edged sword... *Mind Renewal* encapsulates Biblical principles in teaching us how to emancipate ourselves from mental slavery and walk into our divine purpose as children of the Most High God...I'm no longer a slave and the book serves as a Bible to me.

Monique Anderson-Coke
Educational Psychologist

....

As I read chapter seven on "Cracked Performers" the LORD perfected some things that the enemy was using to buffet me. My mind was renewed. I thought my cracks were too much for God to use me but I realize God has used me nonetheless, and I have been effective all along despite being cracked. Nothing about my cracks that the enemy has been using against me will work anymore. This book is my new medicine.

Wendy Lawson-Stephens
Secretary

This book is dedicated to Mrs. Loraine Watson-Dean, my 88-year old grandmother. I looked forward to spending every holiday with you. I enjoyed the daily trips to the Rocky Point Market where you sold your wares. But most memorable are the words that I still embrace to this day when you said to me: "You are not my grandson, you are my son." Love you, Granny…

INTRODUCTION

The mind is the factory where the decision of victory or defeat, poverty or wealth is conceived and pursued. It is easily the most valuable asset of one's possessions. One of the best gifts given to man by God is the ability to think. The dimension of one's thoughts is manifested daily through spoken words and deeds. This position is substantiated by Proverbs 23:7a, which reads, "As a man thinks in his heart so his he."

Unfortunately, many minds are bankrupted with low level processing which produces unacceptable speech and actions. A depraved mind will serve as a barricade to new opportunities. There are possibilities that remain unknown because they reside outside of the parameters of healthy or renewed thinking.

This devotional series was birthed from the book, *Mind Renewal: Biblical Secrets to a Better You*. I truly believe that one of the greatest self-investment to be pursued is the renewing of your mind. This is volume 1 of a three-part series.

According to Romans 12:2, we should not conform to the world but rather be transformed by the renewing of our mind. The evidence of Mind Renewal will be heard and seen as daily transformation is pursued.

This 30-Day *Mind Renewal Transformation Devotional* serves as a vehicle to your transformation. This volume has five parts which cover topics dealing with the wealth of criticism, having a great mind, investing in your future and the power of the word.

Use it alongside the *Mind Renewal* book. This devotional is equipped with transforming stories, supporting scriptures, assignments and a daily journal page. The journal page is to be used to document your daily assignments, challenges and victories. I would advise you not to move on to another day before completing the assignments and journal of the present one.

Get ready to become a better you!

TABLE OF CONTENTS

PART 1: THE WEALTH OF CRITICISM 1

    Day 1: Work the Criticism 1

    Day 2: Critique Me Until I'm My Best Me 5

    Day 3: The Ladder that Goes Up also Goes Down 9

    Day 4: Celebrate Your Success 13

    Day 5: Growth Restrictions 17

    Day 6: Not Everyone Has the Same Sky 21

    Day 7: Partner in Your Success 25

PART II: INVEST IN YOUR FUTURE 29

    Day 8: Know Your Past, Secure Your Future 31

    Day 9: From Past to the Future 35

    Day 10: Futuristic Deposits 39

    Day 11: Speak Positively into Your Future 43

    Day 12: Partner with Your Declared Future 47

    Day 13: No Place for Fear 51

    Day 14: God is Your Future 55

PART III: GREAT MINDS 59

Day 15: Fear of Failing 61
Day 16: Mind Expansion 67
Day 17: Wealthy Spirits Seek Wealth 71
Day 18: Reject Low Grounds 75
Day 19: Mind for Service 79
Day 20: Great Minds and Systems of Injustice ..83
Day 21: Demonstrate Your Belief 87

PART IV: THE POWER OF WORDS 91

Day 22: Promise: Established Truth 93
Day 23: Use Your Authority 97
Day 24: Command Knowing it's Done 101
Day 25: Creative Tongue 105
Day 26: Don't to Do It Your Way 109
Day 27: The Between 113
Day 28: Promise-Suicide 117

PART V:: IT STARTS WITH YOU 121

Day 29: Let the Change Begin with You 123
Day 30: Failing and Re-starting 127
Acknowledgements 133

About the Author.. 134

PART 1:

THE WEALTH OF CRITICISM

Day 1

WORK THE CRITICISM

Scripture: Mark 2: 10-17

Criticism is inevitable. Jesus was having dinner at Matthew's house. Ma- ny tax collectors and sinners came and ate with Him and His disciples. When the Pharisees saw this, they asked His disciples, "Why does your teacher eat with tax collectors and sinners?" On hearing this, Jesus said, "Those who are well have no need of a physician but those who are sick" (Mark 2: 17a).

You don't have control over what people say to you or about you, nor what they do to you, but you have control over your response or reaction. In the Department of Social

Services where I am employed, there is a feedback form. Clients are asked to complete it before leaving. This is used to assist the Department in its improvement. In High School someone told Peron that he smelled mouldy. He was embarrassed and decided never to wear a dirty uniform to school again. This resulted in him becoming more aware of his appearance; his self-esteem improved and the criticism positioned him to a better place.

Your response determines if you become broken or empowered. Jesus was not exempt from criticism but He never shied away from it. Don't allow criticisms to derail you from your purpose. Follow Jesus' example. He worked their criticism of Him to highlight His assignment.

ASSIGNMENT

1. Reminisce and record how you handled your last critique.

2. Record how you handled your first criticism after reading Day 1.

Document your responses to the assignment as well as your challenges and victories.

_____

_____

_____

THE WEALTH OF CRITICISM

MIND RENEWAL TRANSFORMATION DEVOTIONAL

Day 2

CRITIQUE ME UNTIL I'M MY BEST ME

Scripture: James 1:19

Viewing criticism in a negative light is the preferred choice, however, if that continues, we will miss the wealth of being critiqued. The easiest route does not necessarily equate to the best. The University of the West Indies was criticized by journalist Wilmot Perkins, as being an *Intellectual Ghetto,* and they used it as a weapon of transformation.

You should view criticism as stones being thrown at you. These stones must then be gathered and used to construct a needed empire. Use that empire to serve all including the *stone-throwers.* At that point you can say, "It was good that I was critiqued." Stop wasting the raw materials you have been freely given. Notice, you don't have to purchase or fetch the criticisms, they are freely given to you. A renewed mind position is to express good mannerism. If someone gives you something, you express your gratitude. Be thankful to those who bless you with criticism.

James said, "Let every man be swift to hear, slow to speak, slow to wrath" (James 1:19). Rather than be angry at a critic, let us be "quick to listen. Swiftness to anger can be the tool used to rob us of the wealth of that criticism. Let this be your renewed motto: *Critique me until I'm my best me.*

ASSIGNMENT

1. List one criticism you did not maximize.
2. Prepare and strategize in writing how you will approach your next criticism. When it happens, document how differently you dealt with it.

Document your responses to the assignment as well as your challenges and victories.

_____

_____

_____

_____

_____

_____

THE WEALTH OF CRITICISM

MIND RENEWAL TRANSFORMATION DEVOTIONAL

Day 3

THE LADDER THAT GOES UP ALSO GOES DOWN

Scripture: Acts 1: 11

The same ladder that takes you up, takes you down. Be clear on the location of your destiny. Be willing to not be driven by the movement of the crowd but by the direction of your destiny. Neither the crowd nor the news is your compass. For example, education has been used as a very effective tool in elevation from poverty but has been used as a vehicle by which humans are carried away from God. Persons have pulled away from faith and into intellect and logic. There are times when they are enemies. Human logic says a virgin cannot give birth, man cannot walk on water neither can the dead be called back to life. But faith says, nothing is impossible for God.

After His resurrection, Jesus ascended and angels from heaven spoke, "Men of Galilee, why do you stand gazing up into heaven? This *same* Jesus, who was taken up from you into heaven, will so come in like manner as you saw Him go into heaven" (Acts 1:11, NKJV). Jesus retained authority over His direction. He went up and will come back down. Whatever aspect of your life has gone down, be it health, finances or marriage, be cognizant of this truth: *The ladder was not burnt, it is still in place and climbing up is still a viable option.*

ASSIGNMENT

Write down the areas that are presently down in your life and develop an upward plan for each. Be committed to the plan. Work it.

Document your responses to the assignment as well as your challenges and victories.

_____

_____

_____

_____

_____

_____

THE WEALTH OF CRITICISM

Day 4

CELEBRATE YOUR SUCCESS

Scripture: 2 Samuel 6:16-21

Many persons have plummeted into depression because they were not recognized or celebrated for a good deed done. However, we must stop expec- ting everyone to celebrate our success. Remove yourself from waiting for others to show appreciation, instead, spread your own red carpet. You laboured and committed to going against the flow of mediocrity and employed the spirit of excellence. Celebrate your achievements! Celebrate you! We celebrate independence, emancipation, birthdays, anniversaries and that's all good. But when is celebrate me day? As you travel on this journey of Mind Renewal begin with the celebration of your small achievements. Then evolve into the majors. Finally, make a full celebrate me day. Celebrate your past and present victories and I dare you to celebrate your not so victorious memories. Remember, if you learned anything from your down situations, you actually gained. That's cause for celebration.

King David in the book of Samuel succeeded in returning the Ark of the Covenant to the House of David and he celebrated. His celebration was meted with disgust from Saul's daughter. Remember, as you celebrate your success, not everyone will be rejoicing with you. Refrain from being daunted by their poverty. Let not the insecurities or the rejections of your peers block you from celebrating each milestone you have conquered. Be determined to celebrate you with all your faculties. Rejoice, by the grace of God, you have achieved

ASSIGNMENT

Develop an attitude of celebration. Commence with celebrating your last major or minor achievement. Be it ten years of marriage, acquiring your degree or resisting a temptation. Celebrate!

Document your responses to the assignment as well as your challenges and victories.

MIND RENEWAL TRANSFORMATION DEVOTIONAL

THE WEALTH OF CRITICISM

Day 5

GROWTH RESTRICTIONS

Scripture: Acts 23: 1-10

Many possibilities have remained un-ventured simply because they reside outside of the parameters of a person's belief system. The expanse of a man's sky will never outgrow the restrictions of his belief system. A depraved self-world-view will serve as a barricade to new possibilities.

A belief is something we consider to be a fact. It is anything that we assume to be true. Your belief system is used to comprehend life. They serve as unintentional autopilots. Once formulated, these beliefs become entrenched in us.

THE WEALTH OF CRITICISM

A popular adage is, "seeing is believing." We were raised to accept this engraved saying into our belief system. However, without much consideration, this has been proven to not be true. We are not privileged to see our thoughts from which our actions flow, yet we know they are real. This means making well needed adjustments to our belief system. In Acts chapter 23: 8, we see that the Sadducees did not believe in the resurrection of the dead nor in the existence of angels or spirits, but the Pharisees believed in both. Paul finding himself in a tight place between both sects, used their different belief systems against them for his escape. Neither of the two groups was able to look beyond the boundaries of their belief system.

ASSIGNMENT

Question your core beliefs. Are they the complete truth? If not begin to modify.

Document your responses to the assignment as well as your challenges and victories.

_____

_____

_____

_____

_____

MIND RENEWAL TRANSFORMATION DEVOTIONAL

Day 6

NOT EVERYONE HAS THE SAME SKY

Scripture: John 14:12

Frequently you hear the following words being echoed, "The sky is the limit." However, this poses a question: "Does everyone have the same sky?" Each man's sky is the representation of the opportunities, resources and outlets available at his disposal. Is the sky the same for those in the Philippines whose meal is Pagpag as those in the USA who eat ribs and steaks? Pagpag is a term given to left-over food, meat picked from garbage and dumps, which is then washed, cooked and sold to poor communities in Manila, Philippines. This is their daily staple food.

It is obvious that not everyone has the same economic, political or social sky. What is however more important than the equality of skies is the effective use of one's sky. T.D. Jakes once said, "There are persons who have done more with less than those with plenty." Each person must ensure the maximization of the sky that is presented before them. Don't stop climbing until you have reached the roof of your sky. When that happens, you will realize that was not the limit but a new opening to be unlocked. The only equal sky available is from Jesus. He said, "Most assuredly, I say to you, he who believes in Me, the works that I do he will do also; and greater *works* than these he will do, because I go to My Father" (John 14:12).

ASSIGNMENT

1. Look at the opportunities you have not maximized. Change that.
2. Revisit the works of Jesus. Pursue to first do the same and then the greater works.

Document your responses to the assignment as well as your challenges and victories.

_____

_____

_____

_____

_____

THE WEALTH OF CRITICISM

MIND RENEWAL TRANSFORMATION DEVOTIONAL

Day 7

PARTNER IN YOUR SUCCESS

Scripture: Nehemiah 6:1-4

One of the most repeated quotes of all time is, "The heights by great men reached and kept were not attained by sudden flight, but they, while their companions slept, were toiling upward in the night" (Henry Wadsworth Longfellow). What is your role in your victory or success? According to Longfellow, your success will not be found on the plains of sleeping nor by sudden flight but from the rigorousness of one's ability to pursue where others have faltered. The determination to not give in to the loud screaming of your body as it calls out for sleep, must be given priority as you keep focused on the victory that awaits you.

In the book of Nehemiah, we see where he got permission from the King to return to Jerusalem and rebuild the breaches of the city. This was met with opposition which came in the disguise of friendliness. He discerned that the opposition intended evil towards him. When they requested him to meet with them, he responded, "So, I sent messengers to them, saying, "I *am* doing a great work, so that I cannot come down. Why should the work cease while I leave it and go down to you?" (Nehemiah 6:3). Nehemiah understood he must remain focused on the success that awaited him. He was determined not to permit any source of derailment to succeed. He partnered with his success. He went on to complete his project successfully.

ASSIGNMENT

No more settling for average. Be fervent in prayer asking God for the grace to attain and keep the heights that only few achieve.

Document your responses to the assignment as well as your challenges and victories.

___

___

___

___

___

THE WEALTH OF CRITICISM

MIND RENEWAL TRANSFORMATION DEVOTIONAL

PART II:

INVEST IN YOUR FUTURE

Day 8

KNOW YOUR PAST, SECURE YOUR FUTURE

Scripture: Judges 6:15

To effectively navigate oneself into the wealth of the future, one must have intimate knowledge of where one is coming from. The multilingualism of your past is daily shouting to your future as the fight for success or failure rages daily. The negatives of your past, if not tamed or controlled, can bully your present and future into maintaining the status of poverty. When John looked at his past he saw infidelity, divorce, gambling, children out of wedlock and ministry. It was too late for his first marriage which was already broken but early for his second. John equipped with knowledge, prayed effectively to silence the negatives of the past and promote the positives. He prayed not only for himself but also his children.

Gideon in Judges 6: 15 spoke from what he inherited. He was not in a place to receive what the angel had released to him when he called him, "a mighty man of valour." Gideon's response was that his family was the least and that he was the least in his family. The past said, *Gideon you will not amount to anything great*, but the Angel said, "Your future is mighty." Many languages are spoken daily but each person must decide which language will be adhered to.

ASSIGNMENT

1. Pursue mastery in identifying and responding to the multilingualism of your past.

2. Stop allowing the negatives of the past to determine your present and future.

3. Make a list of where you have been bullied by your past. Then pursue overriding the verdict handed to you.

Document your responses to the assignment as well as your challenges and victories.

_____

_____

INVEST IN YOUR FUTURE

MIND RENEWAL TRANSFORMATION DEVOTIONAL

Day 9

FROM PAST TO THE FUTURE

Scripture: Exodus 16:3

There is a repeated mistake of persons abiding in their past experiences and miss the present and future possibilities. While we embrace and learn from the successes and failures of the past, we must never resign in the place of memory. The children of Israel were delivered from slavery and journeyed to the Promised Land. They encountered challenges and a repeated sentiment to Moses was, "why didn't you leave us in Egypt?" They were physically out of Egypt but their minds were trapped there.

If your mind is not emancipated, it will never allow you to bask in the present and the future. Didn't we tell you this would happen while we were still in Egypt? We said, "Leave us alone! Let us be slaves to the Egyptians. It's better to be a slave in Egypt than a corpse in the wilderness! If only the LORD had killed us back in Egypt," they moaned. "There we sat around pots filled with meat and ate all the bread we wanted. But now you have brought us into this wilderness to starve us all to death." Thomas Jefferson said, "I like the dreams of the future better than the history of the past."

For too long we have allowed the past to paralyze and bankrupt our future through our failure to move on physically and mentally. Now we are going forward, forsaking the past. It might be a broken relationship, failed business, bad treatment from parents and family... It's time to move on.

ASSIGNMENT

Do a deep soul search. List the areas where you are stuck. Get an accountable partner and pursue newness by letting go. Address one area at a time.

Document your responses to the assignment as well as your challenges and victories.

_____

_____

_____

_____

_____

MIND RENEWAL TRANSFORMATION DEVOTIONAL

INVEST IN YOUR FUTURE

Day 10

FUTURISTIC DEPOSITS

Scripture: Genesis 41:47-49

The disjointment of the past, present, and future that is desired by many is not completely possible because there is continuity in our living. We must be conscious of this reality; we are coexisting in the present and the future simultaneously. What we are living today are actually the choices of yesterday, and tomorrow we will weep or rejoice at decisions we make today.

The perceived achievements of the unfulfilled will not be attained by much sleep or slumber but by consistency and determination towards the desired results. We must be willing to aggressively and systematically pursue tomorrow today. For this to be realized, sacrifices must be made.

In Genesis 41, we see a classical example of preparing for the future in the present. Pharaoh had a dream that troubled him. Joseph's interpretation of Pharaoh's dream required investment in the present to secure a healthy future for the nation of Egypt. Egypt was going to experience seven years of plenty then seven years of famine. Wisdom dictated that preparation be made during the time of plenty for the period of lack. Let us stop living just for the now.

ASSIGNMENT

1. What is the future you envision for yourself and family? Prayerfully calculate and prepare a plan to achieve your big goal.

2. Make smaller attainable time-frame goals, which lead to the main one. Work it.

Document your responses to the assignment as well as your challenges and victories.

_____

_____

_____

_____

_____

_____

INVEST IN YOUR FUTURE

MIND RENEWAL TRANSFORMATION DEVOTIONAL

Day 11

SPEAK POSITIVELY INTO YOUR FUTURE

Scripture: Proverbs 18:21

Recently I was engaged in a conversation with a father who told me his sons (three and four years old) will not do well educationally, and so he wants to get them into learning mechanics. The mother interjected and said, "They are doing well in school now." Without realizing, he was prophesying negatively into the future of his children. Jesus demonstrated how to speak into your future. "I'm going to die, but on the third day, I shall rise." Now, this is a bold and serious futuristic investment.

Jesus demonstrated to us the power of orchestrating the future while we are still living in the present. His words decided the chain of events that he would experience in the near future. He dictated the order. Killed, then resurrected. Jesus was not the only one who spoke and changed the future; God the Father did it also.

In Genesis 1:1-3, we read,

> In the beginning God created the heaven and the earth. And the earth was without form, and void; and darkness was upon the face of the deep. And the Spirit of God moved upon the face of the waters. And God said, 'Let there be light: and there was light.'

The state of the earth never changed until God spoke. His spoken word brought about a new reality- light. Darkness reigned until light appeared at the spoken word. When God spoke, He changed the course of the future. It shifted from a period of continuous darkness to one that embraced light. It is said, a closed mouth is closed blessings, an open mouth opens either blessings or curse. Life and death are in the mouth. Choose life.

ASSIGNMENT

Make a concerted effort to speak positively into every area of your life and reject every negative that is spoken.

Document your responses to the assignment as well as your challenges and victories.

MIND RENEWAL TRANSFORMATION DEVOTIONAL

INVEST IN YOUR FUTURE

Day 12

PARTNER WITH YOUR DECLARED FUTURE

Scripture: 1 Samuel 17: 22-50

In 2012 Maxine developed asthma and received asthmatic inhalers and medication from her doctor. In January of 2013, she went into fasting and on the first day, heard the Spirit of the Lord say, "You are healed." She completely believed. In demonstrating her partnership with the Lord, she immediately threw out the tablets and the inhalers. Faith was activated in securing her future. Since then she has never had any further asthmatic problems.

The patriot David demonstrated this also in 1 Samuel 17. When David fought against Goliath, he prophesied to his enemy how the matter will unfold. David then ran towards the change he prophesied. Look at his attitude! He ran towards... As we renew our minds, our attitude must also be transformed, which can mean being in a different place from the crowd which surrounds you. Prior to David's arrival, the soldiers of the army of Israel ran from Goliath, but David had a renewed mindset which propelled him to run towards the enemy. The soldiers saw a mighty man of war, David envisioned a dead, headless uncircumcised Philistine. His victory began with his perception.

Some have been declaring, prophesying but not partnering with their prophesied future. This needs to change. If you desire it, declare it and partner with it! You partner with faith by works. Get involved and pursue the desired future. For example, if you want your degree, go to school.

ASSIGNMENT

If you have declared it but have not partnered with it, make the change now.

Document your responses to the assignment as well as your challenges and victories.

_____
_____
_____

INVEST IN YOUR FUTURE

MIND RENEWAL TRANSFORMATION DEVOTIONAL

Day 13

NO PLACE FOR FEAR

Scripture: 1Samuel 17: 8-11

In April of 2019, a friend called me on the telephone. She was at work and wanted to take a nap on her lunch break. She went to the rest area but a lizard was at the door post. Fear of the lizard gripped her and prevented her from getting the well needed rest. Truth is, there are a variety of things that persons are afraid of. Some are afraid of the dark, pain, closed space and the list goes on. Fear is equipped with the resources to cripple an individual, family or nation.

In 1 Samuel 17, the soldiers of the Army of Israel were afraid of Goliath and fled. But the brave David rejected fear and spoke boldly to the enemy. He made three promises to his enemy/situation and he delivered on his words. He told the enemy, *I'm going to cut off your head, without having a sword for himself.* After killing him, David ran and stood over him. He took hold of the Philistine's sword and drew it from the sheath and cut off his head with his own sword.

As you renew your mind, be cognizant of this truth, not all that you will need to accomplish that which you desire, must necessarily be owned by you. Folly is the belief that any one person is self-sufficient. David told Goliath, in order for me to fulfill my promise to you, I will use your own resources. You will not be in a position to prevent me, so I'm just letting you know.

Fear is a bully! You must take a stance and bully the bully. For too long fear has been dancing on the comfort of our minds, preventing some of us from even sleeping. But it is just time for fear to know there is no place for it. You are pursuing the change of no longer being a slave to fear.

ASSIGNMENT

Make a list of your fears. Select two and work on their elimination.

Document your responses to the assignment as well as your challenges and victories.

INVEST IN YOUR FUTURE

MIND RENEWAL TRANSFORMATION DEVOTIONAL

Day 14

GOD IS YOUR FUTURE

Scripture: Jeremiah 29:11

A young devout Christian male worked as a High School teacher and was one year short of being qualified for retirement. Then the Lord spoke to him telling him to quit his job and go to Seminary. He decided to submit to the will of God. This meant leaving his birth land to study in another country. While he prepared to leave, his mother became sick, his father had a surgery to be done and his brother had a mental break down. Yet, the Lord told him to leave immediately. "No delays, leave now."

He came under scrutiny not just from the secular world but also from the Christian community. How can you abandon your family in this time of crisis? However, the young man was fully persuaded that God was his captain and He must be obeyed. He was convinced God would take care of his family better than he could ever imagine. So he left, and God took care of his family. They were all healed.

Like the young man, we should fulfill the instruction of Hebrews 12:2 which states, "Looking unto Jesus the author and finisher of our faith; who for the joy that was set before him endured the cross, despising the shame, and is set down at the right hand of the throne of God." The cross for the young man was the persecution by family and friends. But the joy that outweighed the cross was being obedient to God who holds the future. He decided God is my future and what my future says, that I will obey.

Today he is married and pastoring a church. The young man trusted God being fully persuaded of Jeremiah 29:11: "For I know the thoughts that I think toward you, says the LORD, thoughts of peace and not of evil, to give you a future and a hope." A great position to be in is total submission to God who is your future. The Bible declares," the steps of a righteous man are ordered by the Lord" Psalms 37:23).

ASSIGNMENT

Let's reflect. Where have you failed in submitting to the will of God? If it's not too late, get it rectified. If too late, prepare for the next request from God.

INVEST IN YOUR FUTURE

Document your responses to the assignment as well as your challenges and victories.

MIND RENEWAL TRANSFORMATION DEVOTIONAL

PART III:
GREAT MINDS

Day 15

FEAR OF FAILING

Scripture: Matthew 14: 22-31

The fear of failing has contributed immensely to true potentials not being realized. When I attended the Jamaica Evangelistic Centre in Jamaica, Careen Baker corrected me after I uttered, "I'm going to work for my slice of the cake." She replied, "Why only a slice? Why not work to own the bakery?" Motivational Speaker Les Brown said it this way, "Most people fail in life not because they aim too high and miss, but because they aim too low and hit." Achieving the slice of cake for some would be a success but for others a huge failure. All seats occupied means a fruitful event but not necessarily a successful host. Achievement below your true potential is failure.

According to Matthew 14: 29, Peter began walking on the water but started to sink before reaching his destination, which was Jesus. Peter achieved what no other disciple was credited in doing and while we applaud him for his faith in stepping out of his norm, we cannot ignore his failure. He failed not because he did not achieve anything, but because his achievement fell below his true potential. His true potential would have seen him standing beside Jesus or even walking with Jesus on the water.

ASSIGNMENT

1. Make a list of three projects that you accomplished but because your pass grade was set low, you're now seeing that you failed. Examine thoroughly and cite where you could have strived for greater.

2. For a present or future assignment, increase the goals. Work towards your new high goals.

Document your responses to the assignment as well as your challenges and victories.

_____

_____

GREAT MINDS

MIND RENEWAL TRANSFORMATION DEVOTIONAL

GREAT MINDS

Day 16

MIND EXPANSION

Scripture: Genesis 12:1-3

I listened to an invited speaker address the host pastor and he highlighted the mind of the founder of the church. He said, "The size of your auditorium (100-seater) expresses where your spirit took you, as you planned and executed your vision." The truth is, the journey of your spirit determines the heights and depth of your expectations.

You will never tread the paths your mind has not gone. The founder was not allowed to go beyond a hundred (100) seats because that's where his spirit or vision stopped. A major failure would be, residing at the place of your spirit's first stop. There must be continuation which will see your spirit discovering new terrains. As expansion and expectation take place in your spirit, there must be a matching expansion and expectation in your physical domain. This is to facilitate the increase.

God said to Abram in Genesis 12, leave all that you know and I will establish and make you a great nation. Your name will be great and you will become a blessing. Abram's spirit upon hearing the words of Jehovah had to travel the path of the spoken words. Abram believed and pursued.

Abram's nephew Lot and his family received instructions from three angels to leave their home and flee to the mountains because the place would be destroyed. They started the journey but Lot's wife's spirit failed to pursue. Her spirit returned to what it knew. This resulted in her demise. As you continue on the journey of life, please understand that there will always be new territories to discover. Refuse to fail because you closed your spirit to expansion.

ASSIGNMENT

1. Have you conquered all godly terrains that your spirit has explored?
2. What about that dream or vision of increase? Time now to pursue.

Document your responses to the assignment as well as your challenges and victories.

_____

_____

MIND RENEWAL TRANSFORMATION DEVOTIONAL

GREAT MINDS

Day 17

WEALTHY SPIRITS SEEK WEALTH

Scripture: Genesis 26: 1-33

When I studied at the Jamaica Theological Seminary, we had an assignment to complete a genogram. A genogram is a graphic representation of a family tree that displays detailed data on relationships among individuals. It goes beyond a traditional family tree by allowing the user to analyze hereditary patterns and psychological factors that punctuate relationships. It was brutally challenging for some; so much so, one young lady quit her studies. While for others, it was the prescription needed to commence their healing.

Persons were exposed to deep family patterns that were affecting their functionality. I learned that a wealthy spirit will prosper where mediocre minds perish. The same terrain produces different results. The results of your peers are not an indication of what you will accomplish but rather the state of your spirit. A wealthy spirit seeks wealth in every situation, not just the good times. Wealthy spirits believe consistently the words of Romans 8:28: "And we know that all things work together for good to them that love God, to them who are called according to his purpose." Isaac had a wealthy spirit which propelled him to sow in the time of famine. While others were experiencing the menace of the famine, he saw opportunity. That year he reaped a hundredfold.

ASSIGNMENT

1. Do a genogram. Pay attention to the patterns of the past. Do prayer and fasting against all negative patterns.

2. Evaluate the state of your mind by how you have responded to various terrains.

3. If you are at a mediocre place invest in your improvement. If you are at a wealthy place, seek greater.

Document your responses to the assignment as well as your challenges and victories.

MIND RENEWAL TRANSFORMATION DEVOTIONAL

MIND RENEWAL TRANSFORMATION DEVOTIONAL

Day 18

REJECT LOW GROUNDS

Scripture: Judges 6:12-22

In 2018, the Lord told me that I was asking too low. I realized I was restrained from making any request that was above my frequency of thinking. A beautiful, independent Christian single girlfriend of mine expressed the desire to get married. I knew a male friend who was single, financially stable and a Christian who was also seeking marriage. I shared her photo with him and was truly disappointed at his response. He said, "She is too beautiful for me." His low ground of mental abode shackled him. He is still single and searching within the parameters of his low thinking.

The Bible tells us, "For as he thinks in his heart, so is he" (Proverbs 23:7). Here lies the problem: we have not stretched our minds to inhabit high frequencies of thinking but have settled at low grounds. Rather than learning to fly across the open fields, we crawl among petals of green. In Judges 6, the Angel of the Lord told Gideon that He was sending him to save Israel from the hand of the Midianites.

Gideon responded that his family was poor and he was the least in his family. Gideon's frequency of thinking did not allow him to receive with gladness what the angel said. The angel by his words promoted Gideon to the place of a Judge but he was stuck at being the least. Where has your thinking bound you? It is high time to reject the low grounds.

ASSIGNMENT

Pursue a deep revamping of your thinking processor. Begin to think according to the word of God. Be warned, you're about to be transformed.

Document your responses to the assignment as well as your challenges and victories.

_____

_____

_____

_____

_____

_____

MIND RENEWAL TRANSFORMATION DEVOTIONAL

GREAT MINDS

Day 19

MIND FOR SERVICE

Scripture: Luke 6: 36

In 2017, I heard a guest speaker at a conference say, "he wants to go the grave empty." At first glance I thought, "That's nothing deep, as we all go to the grave empty." However, as he expounded, I realized he spoke of emptying his great mind in service to the Lord and his fellow humans. Many persons have contributed to making the cemetery the wealthiest place on earth. They died with books, movies, poems, business ventures, ministries, and other world-changing ideas that remained locked up in their minds. What they did not know was, you will never know the true capacity of your reservoir.

However, you will be exposed to depths and heights of what you contain as you empty yourself. The more you release, the more you will receive to continue giving. A great mind will always have and desire to give of its reservoir. Giving of oneself is like a well-defined system of replenishing and expansion. If you want to have more, give more. You will never be able to empty the reservoir of a renewed mind.

Give, and it will be given to you: good measure, pressed down, shaken together, and running over will be put into your bosom. For with the same measure that you use, it will be measured back to you (Luke 6:68).

A minister was sharing with some friends and the Holy Spirit downloaded knowledge into his spirit. It was so powerful, he thought of keeping this knowledge to himself but he decided to share. Immediately as he began sharing the knowledge, new revelation about a different subject began to be downloaded into his spirit. He gave and was replenished.

ASSIGNMENT

Expansion is continued as you serve. Look at three persons or groups to serve and serve them to the best of your ability.

Document your responses to the assignment as well as your challenges and victories.

GREAT MINDS

MIND RENEWAL TRANSFORMATION DEVOTIONAL

Day 20

GREAT MINDS AND SYSTEMS OF INJUSTICE

Scripture: Matthew 14:1-11

Dr. King's great mind refused to accept the inhumane and repulsive belief that one race was superior to another. He spoke of change: a change where all men are treated as created from the same mind— the mind of **God.** Great minds are not afraid to go against the system of injustice, even if it cost them their earthly lives. This was true in King's case. King was assassinated on April 4th, 1968.

John the Baptist demonstrated a great mind and it cost him his life. The account of his death is recorded in Matthew chapter 14. Herod the Tetrarch had taken his brother's wife, Herodias, and John was bold enough to condemn his actions. Herod imprisoned him and then had him killed upon the request of Herodias' daughter.

We were raised in an era, where the informant is stigmatized and his actions are deemed as a grave evil. It's see no evil, hear no evil. The rule is, be silent to the evil that surrounds you. My older brother once said, "The truth is like a bad tooth, it hurts." We must consider the pain of truth or the comfort of a lie. The choice will be presented, to be silent in the stench of injustice or to proclaim the hated truth. You will be the one to carry the burden of silence or the glory of hatred. Which is worth more to you?

ASSIGNMENT

Be adamant: yesterday is the last day you turn a blind eye to injustice. Do your part in stamping out this monster. Someone is depending on your voice. Be silent no more.

Document your responses to the assignment as well as your challenges and victories.

_____
_____
_____
_____

GREAT MINDS

MIND RENEWAL TRANSFORMATION DEVOTIONAL

Day 21

DEMONSTRATE YOUR BELIEF

Scripture: Matthew 17:22-23; 28: 5-9

In democratic societies, every four to five years there are political elections to determine the countries' governance. This is littered with campaign speeches, manifestos and promises. After the victory party is over, the entrusted party has a responsibility to convert their words into actions. The electorate has the right to hold the ruling party to their campaign promises. Their votes were garnered based on those promised words.

Truth is, it is not suffice to only speak. Let your actions be an exact replica of your spoken words. James 2:15-16 states,

If a brother or sister is naked and destitute of daily food, and one of you says to them, "Depart in peace, be warmed and filled," but you do not give them the things which are needed for the body, what *does it* profit?

Jesus not only spoke of His love, but He demonstrated with the ultimate sacrifice: His life. This is the place from which a renewed mind operates. Demonstrate truth and love despite grueling conditions. Jesus is our great example. He declared to His disciples that He will die and be raised on the third day, and He did it. On the third day, the tomb was found empty. Jesus matched His words with His actions.

ASSIGNMENT

Don't be another master of words without actions. But let your words be complimented by matching deeds.

Document your responses to the assignment as well as your challenges and victories.

_____

_____

_____

_____

_____

_____

MIND RENEWAL TRANSFORMATION DEVOTIONAL

PART IV:

THE POWER OF WORDS

Day 22

PROMISE: ESTABLISHED TRUTH

Scripture: Joshua 14:8-13

In early 2019, during family devotion, we discussed promises. My eight-year-old son said I promised to get Lego toys for him and I didn't. I was surprised because I had already explained why he did not get the Lego toys. He saw my actions as a violation to that which was already received in his spirit. Truth is, humans do break promises, but there is a realm where the promised word stands as the established truth. According to Joshua 14:12, Caleb demanded from Joshua the leader, that which was promised to him by Moses. Moses promised Caleb land. When this promise was made to Caleb, a seed was planted. For forty-five years he nurtured it with faith and confidence knowing that once God speaks it, then that's it. It's settled. Hear what Philippians 1: 6 says, "Being confident of this, that he who began a good work in you will carry it on to completion until the day of Christ Jesus."

This great work began by way of a promise. A promise is not just uttered words but within the spirit realm, the land was transferred. When Caleb said, "Give me this mountain that was promised to me," he was in essence saying, I have had this transfer in the spirit realm, now it's time for it to be made manifest in the physical realm. I have the spiritual deed, now I need the physical. Truth is, there are transfers that have been made in the spiritual realm that need to come into our physical coffers.

ASSIGNMENT

Revisit the promises that God has made to you. They are already established. Claim them by faith.

Document your responses to the assignment as well as your challenges and victories.

_____
_____
_____

MIND RENEWAL TRANSFORMATION DEVOTIONAL

THE POWER OF WORDS

Day 23

USE YOUR AUTHORITY

Scripture: Mark 4:36-40

Jesus will not do for you what He has given you the authority to do. The following was said and it had persons in a temporary state of confusion. "God will not do for you what He has empowered you to do." God has endowed you with power. When I attended the International Accelerated Missions Bible School, I witnessed an encounter where the power of command was demonstrated. The class had finished but we were prevented from getting to the parking lot because of a heavy downpour of rain. One teacher, Prophetess Stamp, stood at the doorway, raised her hands to the heavens and commanded the rain to cease and instantly the rain stopped.

Jesus was no stranger to commanding using his authority. In Mark 4:39-40 we see the following:

> Then Jesus got up and rebuked the wind and the sea. "Silence!'" He commanded. "Be still!" And the wind died down, and it was perfectly calm. Jesus then said, "Why are you so afraid?" "Do you still have faith?" Overwhelmed with fear, they (the disciples) asked one another, "Who is this, that even the wind and the sea obey Him?"(Berean Study Bible).

At the beginning of November 2018, the church planned to do a community prayer walk, then came the rain. I remembered to command and exercise my faith and the clouds obeyed my command. Use your God-given authority to command. You're a person of authority, stop acting like a wimp.

ASSIGNMENT

For too long we have been deprived of seeing well needed results. This is because we have not been exercising our authority. Begin to command your day and all that consist of that day.

Document your responses to the assignment as well as your challenges and victories.

MIND RENEWAL TRANSFORMATION DEVOTIONAL

THE POWER OF WORDS

Day 24

COMMAND KNOWING IT'S DONE

Scripture: John 11:1-44

Without faith, the Bible tells us it is impossible to please God. As you embark on a journey of utilizing your authority, you must command in faith. This was modeled for us by Jesus. In John chapter 11, Jesus heard that His friend Lazarus was sick. When Jesus arrived, Lazarus was dead four days. Jesus told them to move the stone from the tomb's mouth. Notice, Jesus did not say, "Come alive," when He called him out of the grave. He said, "Lazarus, come forth."

Upon the announcement of his name, he that was dead responded and then came forth. Jesus said come forth without seeing if Lazarus had responded to his name. That's confidence in one's authority and power. You cannot command doubtingly nor can you wait to see step one fulfilled before commanding step two. Command and believe by faith that it's done.

Bishop Duncan Williams shared an experience. His father who was not a Christian, took him into the yard and showed him a tree that had never given fruit. He spoke to the tree. He said, "Tree if by this time next year, you bear no fruit, I'm cutting you down."

A year later, the tree had on fruit. He spoke to the tree in a threatening commanding manner and the tree responded. After he spoke to the tree, he never went back to remind the tree to see if any changes were happening. He spoke, not doubting and left. This is how Jesus wants us to function. Command by faith and believe it is done.

ASSIGNMENT

No more delay, believe! Increase your faith from believing upon manifestation to command and believe. Put this into practice. Let your new order be: pray, command then thanksgiving by faith.

Document your responses to the assignment as well as your challenges and victories.

MIND RENEWAL TRANSFORMATION DEVOTIONAL

THE POWER OF WORDS

Day 25

CREATIVE TONGUE

Scripture: Matthew 8:5-13

The God you serve speaks and when He speaks elements give way to creation. In the creation account of Genesis, He spoke, and everything came into being. We often times do not know the power that lies in our tongue, and we make the mistake of speaking death instead of life. We have a creative tongue which can either create life or kill it. Whatever we send out in the atmosphere will take shape after a while. Romans 4:17 states, "and call those things which do not exist as though they did."

There is a minister who recounted that as a boy, he would always run from his mother's beatings. One day she said to him, "What a day when your feet fail you." Since then he suffered a broken right leg, torn ankle and knee ligaments of the left foot. And the latest discovery was spurs growing on his ankle bone. He has prayed for the nullification of her uttered words.

In Matthew chapter eight, a centurion approached Jesus asking Him to heal his servant who was at home. Jesus was willing to go the man's house but he said that's not necessary. The centurion had tapped into a higher level of comprehension. He understood that Jesus being a man of authority only needed to speak and His words would create the needed healing.

According to John 10:10, Jesus said, "the thief comes to kill, steal and destroy; I've come that you may have life and have it to the full" (NIV). Your words will either partner with Satan or Jesus. Choose wisely.

ASSIGNMENT

Think about the words that were spoken over your life. Were they words that brought ill? If so, begin to command their nullification now in Jesus' name, and declare the desired outcome. Make notes of the cancellations and the prophecies.

MIND RENEWAL TRANSFORMATION DEVOTIONAL

Document your responses to the assignment as well as your challenges and victories.

THE POWER OF WORDS

Day 26

DON'T TO DO IT YOUR WAY

Scripture: 2 Kings 4:15-17

The Shunamite woman in 2 Kings 4:15-17 was childless and received a prophetic word that she would bring forth a child. She received the promise and despite the odds against her husband (he was old), she understood that he was the only promised helper that must be employed. In other words, the promise did not give her the right to step out of the covenant because the covenant had issues. Challenges are not license to do it your way. God's way must be and remain the only way. Every promise comes with parameters. A challenge we face is our constant desire to help God.

Stemming from a state of several failed relations, divorce and bleeding for a breakthrough, Elizabeth received a prophetic word, that this year would be her best year. She believed the word but approached it wrongfully. Instead of waiting for the leading of the Holy Spirit, she decided she was going to make it happen. She sought destiny helpers who were not assigned to her. She saw the challenges and decided to fix them through fleshy means. Through her effort, she created a worse situation. The challenges associated with the promise are not license to do it your way. What Elizabeth failed to grasp was: *it's in the pursuit of doing it God's way you encounter the miracles.*

ASSIGNMENT

Repent where you did it your way. Submit completely to God's directives, then partner with Him and wait on the promises of God.

Document your responses to the assignment as well as your challenges and victories.

_____

_____

_____

THE POWER OF WORDS

MIND RENEWAL TRANSFORMAATIONAL DEVOTIONAL

Day 27

THE BETWEEN

Scripture: James 1: 6-7

The period between the promise and the manifestation is critical. It is known as "The In Between." This is where a lot of dreams get aborted. Many persons get lost in "The Between" because they are tired of the waiting. They then try to help God. That's evidence of wavering and doubting the Almighty God. James 1:6-7 says you are to ask in faith, nothing wavering. The man who wavers will not receive anything from the Lord. During "The Between" period, you must be steadfast, vigilant and intentional. Be intentional in seeing the dreams and visions come to pass.

A dear friend of mine saw visions of herself doing ministry. A huge mass of people followed her desiring to hear the word of God. In her period of "The Between," she got involved with a guy, left the faith and got a baby. She is presently finding her way back home. "The Between" period is where you need the support of family and friends. But most importantly, the knowledge that you are not alone, the Holy Spirit is with you.

The Lord told me to attend seminary for four years of study. I remember telling a friend Dian Somerville, I would be taking a break at the next semester because of financial restraints. She said, "When we just met, you told me the Lord sent you to study. Are you saying the God who sent you, is not able to provide for you?" I was in "My Between" period and saw the tuition fees rather than the God who sent me. I re-focused and continued. God paid the tuition fees.

ASSIGNMENT

Whatever "dreams and visions have drowned in "The Between" period? It is time to resurrect them. Refocus your lenses by looking at the Almighty God, the one who sustains you, rather than looking at what you do not have.

Document your responses to the assignment as well as your challenges and victories.

_____

_____

THE POWER OF WORDS

MIND RENEWAL TRANSFORMATION DEVOTIONAL

Day 28

PROMISE-SUICIDE

Scripture: Joshua 21:45

Joshua 21:45 reads, "Not a word failed of any good thing which the LORD had spoken to the house of Israel. All came to pass."

Let us establish an undeniable truth: A promise is not merely words, but the commencement of life. In each promise, lies the seed of what was spoken or written. Nurtured seeds bring forth harvests. Unfortunately, without realizing, there have been daily promised suicides. Without the presence of gallows, needles laden with poison, wrist cutting or drowning, the practice of promise suicide continues to grow.

The sanctity of a promise has lost its value to the culture of adjustment. You can kill a promise without feeling guilty. Now we erroneously ascribe to God what we do and have accepted. This puts us in a challenge of seeing and accepting God for who He is. Yet He remains the promise-keeping God. A friend of mine was accused at work of not performing in accordance with her signed contract (Promise). She knew it was a plot to discredit and terminate her. The Lord sent a word to her. He said "vindicated" (Promise).

After two meetings, she received her termination letter. However, she never wavered. She held on to the promise of God. She appealed the ruling and was vindicated and reinstated. She was presented with the options: to believe or commit promise-suicide. She chose the former and received the fulfillment of the promise.

ASSIGNMENT

Renew your mind to the treasure of a promise. No more promise-suicide. What has God promised you?

Document your responses to the assignment as well as your challenges and victories.

_____

_____

THE POWER OF WORDS

MIND RENEWAL TRANSFORMATION DEVOTIONAL

PART V:

IT STARTS WITH YOU

Day 29

LET THE CHANGE BEGIN WITH YOU

Scripture: Matthew 5: 38-48

The repetitive cry of change needed, amounts to nothing until that change is pursued. Will you be the change? Will change begin with you? The late pop star Michael Jackson did a beautiful song titled, "Man in the Mirror." This title speaks volumes as we understand that the man in the mirror is you, me. It is a direct call for personal introspection and transformation first. This model promotes leading by example. As the leader is transformed, so will the followers. The common practice is to examine one's neighbour while failing to search one's self. Let the change begin with you.

Jesus taught and demonstrated changing the world beginning with himself. In Matthew 5, in his teaching popularly known as the Sermon on the Mount, Jesus said, "You have heard that it was said, "You shall love your neighbor and hate your enemy." But I say to you, do good to those who hate you and pray for those who spitefully use you and persecute you" (Matthew 5:43-44).

These are hard sayings from Jesus. Who can live such teaching? Jesus himself demonstrated the change he taught. According to Luke 23:34, as they crucified him Jesus said, "Father, forgive them; for they know not what they do." And they divided His garments and cast lots."

ASSIGNMENT

Seriously make a concerted effort to be the change. Make peace with old rivals. Do good to those who don't expect you to.

Document your responses to the assignment as well as your challenges and victories.

_____

_____

_____

_____

_____

MIND RENEWAL TRANSFORMATION DEVOTIONAL

IT STARTS WITH YOU

Day 30

FAILING AND RESTARTING

Scripture: Matthew 26:69-75

Jah Cure is a Reggae artist from Jamaica. In November 1998, while driving around Montego Bay, Cure was pulled over by the police and arrested on charges of gun possession, robbery and rape. He was prosecuted before the Gun Court in April 1999, found guilty and sentenced to 15 years in prison. Jah Cure later voiced his hit song, "Behind These Prison Walls" which spoke of the anguish he faced in prison and his regrets. The lyrics spoke of him swearing that he could become a better man. He believed in himself.

Jah Cure failed but did not stay down. He got married in 2011 and had his first child the following year. The person who fails to try again is the one who has truly failed.

Peter, one of the disciples of Jesus failed; not once but three times. Yet Jesus sent for him. Peter took the opportunity to restart and did so effectively. Hs first message saw three thousand souls added to the kingdom of God. God used Peter mightily to spread the Gospel.

Have you failed and are sitting on the couch of defeat? If yes, stay there no more. You have many victories to conquer. Let your previous failures propel you to do better. Become a better you by restarting. The man who fails to restart will never experience victory. Let the better you arise from the ashes of past failures.

ASSIGNMENT

Record the area (s) where you have tried and failed? Stop wallowing in self-pity. Examine carefully the reasons for your failure. Make adjustments and retry.

Document your responses to the assignment as well as your challenges and victories.

_____

_____

_____

MIND RENEWAL TRANSFORMATION DEVOTIONAL

MIND RENEWAL TRANSFORMATION DEVOTIONAL

CONCLUSION

Lao Tzu, a renowned Chinese philosopher said, "The journey of a thousand miles begins with the first step." You commenced your journey of the renewal of your mind with the book, *Mind Renewal: Biblical Secrets to a Better You*. This journey continued with the first of three thirty-day volumes of the *Mind Renewal Transformation Devotional*.

I encourage you to take the next step of this journey with Volume Two of the devotional series. Volume Two delves into topics such as discovering the wealth of serving, living a purpose-driven life, managing your scars and preparing for your next season.

As you continue this intentional pursuit of not conforming to the world, I encourage you with the words of Philippians 1: 6, "Being confident of this very thing, that He who has begun a good work in you will complete it until the day of Jesus Christ." You are not on this Mind Renewal journey alone; the Holy Spirit is there with you to see it into completion.

ACKNOWLEDGEMENTS

To the Holy Spirit my primary Destiny Helper. I was almost finished writing *Mind Renewal: Biblical Secrets to a Better You*, when you said to me early one morning, "Devotional." I was a bit disappointed because I had an unfinished manuscript that I wanted to complete. I obeyed and here we are today. Thank you for being my guide.

Special thanks to my supportive wife, Sherene Morrison, who worked without reservation in editing and proofreading. Your support is invaluable.

Laura Badjnaut, I appreciate you. You willingly gave of your time in fine-tuning.

My friend Hillary Campbell, you ensured I wrote this book. Your encouragement is priceless. I pray every author finds an encourager like you.

A big thank you to the three readers who willingly gave praise reports: Mrs. Wendy Lawson Stephens, Rev. Ramon Douglas and Mrs. Monique Anderson Coke.

To the team at Extra MILE Innovators, you have certainly lived up to your name. You have gone the extra mile without complaint. Thank you.

ABOUT THE AUTHOR

Jamaican born, Rev. Leostone Peron Morrison, is the author of the book, *Mind Renewal: Biblical Secrets to a Better You,* from which this devotional series was birthed. He has served as an Assistant Pastor, Guidance Counselor at the Ministry of Education in Jamaica, and Probation Officer in St Kitts and Nevis.

He is the founder of Next Level Let's Climb Bible Study Ministry. Bathroom cleaning was his first ministry assignment.

Rev. Morrison is a graduate of the Jamaica Theological Seminary and holds a bachelor's degree in Theology, with a minor in Guidance and Counseling. He acquired a diploma in Biblical Principles from Victory Bible School, and a certificate from the International Accelerated Missions School. He is married and has four sons and one daughter.

NOTE: For feedback, consultation or speaking engagements contact Rev. Morrison at restorativeauthor@gmail.com. Kindly submit a review on Amazon or the platform where you bought this book. Thank you.

www.ingramcontent.com/pod-product-compliance
Lightning Source LLC
Chambersburg PA
CBHW071511040426
42444CB00008B/1597